Please return to
Broadview Community UCC
325 N 125th Street
Seattle, WA 98311

Soul Journey
Poetic Expressions
of a Heart-Centered Life

12/08/10

To The people AT BCUCC
MAy you CoNtiNue iN
good health &
Spiritual growth
Judy Ziblell

Soul Journey

Poetic Expressions
of a Heart-Centered Life

Judy Zibbell

Aperion Books

APERION BOOKS™
1611A South Melrose Dr #173
Vista, California 92081
www.AperionBooks.com

Copyright © 2010 by Judy Zibbell

All rights reserved. No part of this book may be reproduced or transmitted in any form or by any means, electronic or mechanical, including photocopying, recordings, or by any information storage and retrieval system, without written permission from the author, except for the inclusion of a brief quotation in a review.

10 9 8 7 6 5 4 3 2
First edition published 2001
Second edition published 2010
Printed in the United States of America

ISBN-10: 0-9829678-2-9
ISBN-13: 978-0-9829678-2-9
Library of Congress Catalog Card Number: 2010914369

Cover & book design by CenterPointe Media
www.CenterPointeMedia.com

Dedication

This book is fondly dedicated to my parents
who, through God, gave me life.

Table of Contents

Preface 11

Meditation 13

Prayer Carkeek Park 15

Red Flowers 17

Summer Stones 19

Trees 21

Thought One ~ Thought Two 23

Yoga 25

The Sabbath 27

Adonai 29

Black 31

Green 33

Blue 35

Paintings 37

One-Minute Timer 39

Thought Wave 41

Homeless 42

A Kiss 45

I Am Made of Light Rain 47

Bliss 49

The Haunted House 51

Leaves 53

Black People Have Beautiful Skin 55

Lighthouse 57

The Leap of Life 59

Music of the Spheres 60

My Blue Trunk 63

Nighttime Manhattan Beach 65

Helen Keller 67

Song of Songs I 68

Song of Songs II 71

Seattle 73

Tea 75

Loneliness 77

D.H. Lawrence 78

Sleep 81

El Amor Brujo	83
The House of Bernarda Alba	84
Blue Green Harmony	87
At Home	89
Vacation	91
Danny Kay	93
The Sperm Whale	95
Night Thoughts	97
Naomi	99
Cell of Silence	101
Tree	103
Evil	105
Yitzhak Rabin	106
Psalm	109
Prayer: Let Me Be Always Near You	111
Prayer of Comfort	113
Helpmate Prayer	115
A Prayer	117
Author Biography	119

Preface

This is my first book of poetry. It was motivated by a deep inspiration to express my feelings on the printed page. Most of the poems are not edited; they simply fell from the pen onto the page.

Poetry is open to everyone: young, old, rich, and poor. It is the act of solidifying thoughts or feelings in any order the writer chooses, which is the gift of poetry—and the fun of it, too. These poems were collected over a period of almost 10 years and were left sitting in a box. I decided to open the box and make these inspirations into a book. They are now gathered here for your enjoyment.

Soul Journey

Meditation

Go into the mountain and meditate
upon the beauty of our world.
The moist earth, the soft grass,
each single blade

Go into the mountain and meditate
upon the beauty of all creation.
The soaring birds, the wildlife,
cottages by the road.

Go into the mountains and meditate
upon the gifts given to man.
His intellect, his body,
and his soul.
Go into the mountains and find
the gift of peace.

Soul Journey
~14~

Prayer Carkeek Park

The trees in heavenly prayer stand,
bending boughs of suppliants
yearning to be nearer Thee;
in quiet stillness we are born.

Soul Journey
~16~

Red Flowers

Blood pulsates thru the body vein,
dancing on my toes,
soaring with eagles;
I touch the sky

I am a flowering tree,
a bushy tailed fox,
a bottlebrush with ribs of fire.
I raise my branches to the sun.
The wind whips thru
scattering my leaves,
but the red flowers remain.

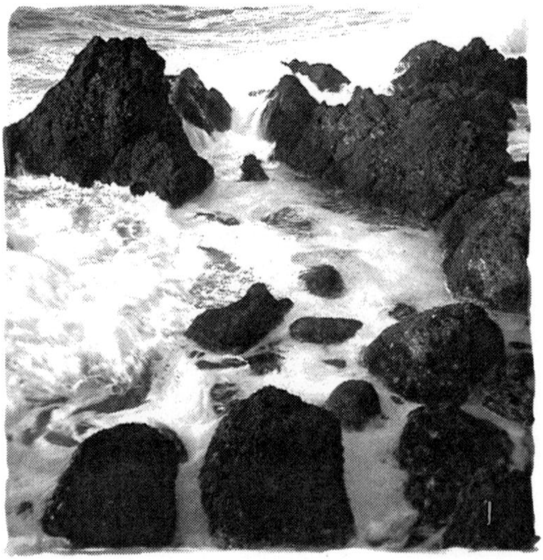

Summer Stones

The quiet dribbling of water over rock.
Sad sunshine filters thru green leaves.
The smooth round rock sits and waits;
sitting thru an eternity of stone;
just waiting till the waters change their course.
The turtle doves fly away and the
ripe red fruit fall among the stones.

Soul Journey

Trees

The trees hug themselves like old friends.
They wrap their winter bark around them
to keep warm in the wintertime.
They kiss their leaves goodbye like
children growing up leave the home.
Now, in the stillness, they kiss each other.

Soul Journey
~22~

Thought One

There is nothing as safe for a woman as the crotch of a tree;
unless it's the groin of her own man.

Thought Two

The difference between a girl and a woman is that the girl
wants to sit safely in the crotch of a tree,
while the woman wants to be inside the groin of her man.

Soul Journey
~24~

Yoga

This morning I sat in yoga. I felt my breath stir inside.
All I could think of were the color of vegetables:
broccoli, split peas.
I am wearing split pea-colored pants.
what are rutabagas?
I think of brussels sprouts and lima beans.
I am angry when I see time passing too quickly.
How soon the life runs out of us.
Insects swarm to our doom.
We waste time pondering over the meaning of life.
It is a vast forest and a rushing water
and we are a blink in the night;
like a cat who slinks off to devour her prey.
I belong to the whole universe.
It is vast and simple.
I am like a rock or a tree.
I walk with my head touching the clouds.
I am friends with my hips and my bones;
I am the universe.

Soul Journey

The Sabbath

We lit candles in the dark,
put them on a raft and sailed them across the swimming pool.
The candles floated in the water.
We said our blessing, and sang about the Sabbath Bride
with long hair down her back.
The braided hallah,
The wine.
I feel peaceful.
That is my Sabbath.

Soul Journey
~28~

Adonai

I am Adonai, the God of anger.
I will rip you to shreds if you disobey me.
I am the God of wrath, spreading destruction
from the valleys to the hills.
I am angry that my children do not love me.
I will throw them into the pit
where they are forsaken.
Better to lose your own mother or father
then be without the sight of God.
I do not forget
though I am merciful.
I rage with fire and thunder.
The hills shake and the trees wither.
My rage is the rage of righteousness.
To hear me is to obey me.
Not to obey me is death.
I chose life.

Soul Journey
~30~

Black

Pitch black inky darkness. Witch's cat. Halloween orange and
black. Witch riding broom. Cat's eyes gleaming
with wickedness. Silky brown fur. Midnight. Witch hazel.
Brown bat's wings. Brown mice. Caves. Blackness of caverns.
Stalactites and stalagmites. Tom Sawyer. Hope is a candle. Fear.
Black Fear. The pit. Pain and suffering. Hidden from God and
light. Suffragettes. Woman and the vote. Right to choice.
Milky way in cold, black solar system. Spaceship.
Light in darkness. Black iron. Cold metal. Steel pipes. Pittsburgh.
Coal dust. Miners. Underground pits. Mud. Clay. Thick boots.
Crust of bread. Pity the workman. Grime and dirt. Pigs.
Farmhouse. Family
Togetherness. Light.

Soul Journey

Green

Thin carpet of grass. Birdseed. Cage in window. Tree outside.
Tall thin branches spreading thin green leaves. Forest.
Birdcalls. More saplings: redwood, birches, firs, evergreen.
Moss on North side of tree. Campers, Hikers.
Hiking stick. Point the way. Childhood green dreams. Light underwater. Green, filmy, fishy, wet coolness of green water.
Lake Louise. One green eye, one blue eye. Strange.
Dreams are green.

Soul Journey

Blue

Ice blue cold water. Frozen lakes and streams. Water, water, water. Wet, cool blueness. Fresh streams, leaping trout. Big oceans, leaping dolphins. Waves crested. Fish flying. Boats out yachting. People in swimsuits sunbathing on board their yachts. Fishing poles and fishermen. Deep blue sea. Calm. Tranquil. Liquid water. Deep blue. Buoys bobbing. People swimming from raft on lake. Vacation with Dulcy. Bathing suits. Black. Stacked. Short. Dulcy. Woman with child. Woman smoking cigarette. Blue water. Flying fish on Grecian vase. Art history class. Blue Forget-me-nots. Poem of flowers and pet rat. Blue Cheer cleaning detergent. Blue. Space in time. Heavens. Gulls circling the sky. Lines of formation of birds. Leader calling. Children look up at sky. Shade eyes from sun.
Golden sun in blue sky. Green grass. The Earth. Stones at my feet. Arch of heaven above. God, Blueness. Eternity.
End and beginning. One.

Soul Journey
~36~

Paintings

My paintings are up
like broad streams.
They carry life within their borders,
colors are in their blood,
movement in their wings.
They beckon me to continue onward
with the thrust of truth
amidst the adventure of life.
Within their frames I am proud and strong.
When I color the canvas,
I color my life.
I allow feelings to enter and flow thru me.
I am sensual and alive.
I am a lover to creation;
I am like a newborn God.

Soul Journey
~38~

One-Minute Timer

We were brought up in life to know everything.
As each day comes and goes.
I learn I know nothing,
and that is exactly the way it should be.

Soul Journey

Thought Wave

We talk about feeding the body,
but how do we feed the mind?
Put morsels of delicate colors slowly
inside the umbilical cord of thought waves.
Recording into the eardrum we
balance the scales
every day.
Can we ever do too much living?

Homeless

Once great land,
homeless speak.
Dark alleyways are hungry.
What have we done or not done?
What can we give that has not been given?
The once proud Statue of Liberty,
"Give me your tired, your poor…"
Does she blush?
Is this the land where dreams come true?
Whose dreams are these that dominate our
landscape (thoughts)?
Wayward youth flash arrogantly by
older people stumble diligently;
making a lump in the stomach
just looking thru the window.
"Keep your eye on the prize".
Shame on you United States.

Lips peel off.
Dung heap.
These are not stones, these are men
talking with their eyes for bread.
Donut and coffee cake;
symbols of gastronomical security.
Cast away on a ship.
Stowaways are treated better than these,
Ishmael's children.
Whose Nobel Prize is this?

Poetic Expressions of a Heart-Centered Life

Soul Journey

A Kiss

Fold me in inky black purple darkness.
Hold me tongue touching, heart throbbing.
Sway with me to the rhythm of your body and mine.
Crash breakers of ocean waves.
Cleanse me with salt spray.
Sink beneath whirling waters
In inky black-blue darkness.
Kiss me.

Soul Journey
~46~

I Am Made of Light Rain

I am made of light rain.
I am made of dark rain.
I am made of 33 flowers budding all the time.
I am made of the full moon soft as glinted sunshine.
I am made of turquoise beads and silver strands.
I am made of golden wheat and blue morning glories.
I am made of 16 trombones and harps and piccolos;
I am made for happiness.

Soul Journey
~48~

Bliss

The body awaits cramped fear.
Fear dying on the rug at my feet as I gingerly pull and push
forward thru the lash of time.
So much time spent wanting not to die
but to live.
Yes, I still read fairy tales.
Princess that I am,
I seek re-assurance from its repetitive pattern.
Good will out.

I remember the stamp, stamp, stamp
of feet in Judaism
No one can control God but we all try.
Wasting time on the defunct ego,
throw him out the window.
Trying so hard to please God
who wants only for me to let go
and be free.

Thinking of treasured sex I want bliss.
Not a moment too soon
I see the sunrise in your eyes
and the warmth and tenderness of a dove's eye.

Soul Journey

The Haunted House

Up the street from where I grew up is a real haunted house.
It has trap doors and a dark face that peers scarily out one of the windows.
There are padlocks on the apartments.
Everything is a low burnt orange color.
The trap doors go down to cellars beneath the apartment.
Ghosts walk thru the corridors at night.
I lost my orange tabby cat there and he became a wild cat who did not know me.
Beware the haunted house.

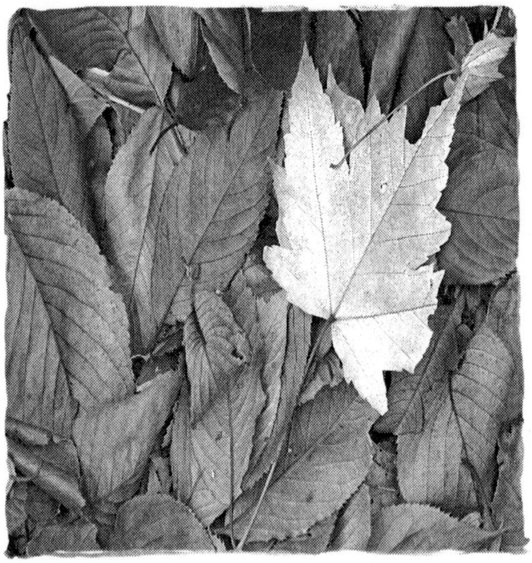

Leaves

Leaves scud across the street.
Leaves drift noiselessly down from yellow-green orange trees.
I rustle thru leaves at my feet;
warm, felt leaves;
dry, scratchy leaves.
September, October, and November leaves.

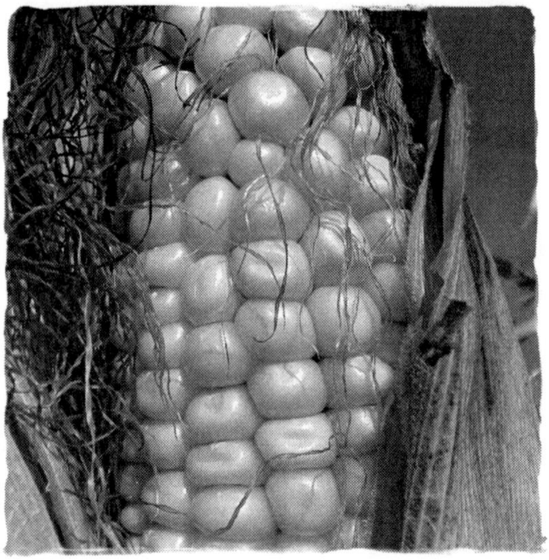

Black People Have Beautiful Skin

Black people have beautiful skin.
It glistens in the sunlight like ripe corn.
It glows in the dark like a candle throbbing to the beat of the African sun.
Their two-toned feet flutter like Japanese lanterns in the breeze.
Sun drenched wires on an electrical line.
I watch the honeybees gather their golden dew
along their paths,
a banquet of flowers.

Soul Journey

Lighthouse

A lighthouse
Standing proud and serene.
Judy in white flannel dress with butterflies on it,
arms uplifted.
Flashing her beacon light over the water,
welcoming travelers
on the wet thunder sea.
A twelve-year-old girl needs a beacon of hope,
a safe harbor, a tower of strength,
as light and life go hand in hand
shedding radiance
like a God in the night.

Soul Journey
~58~

The Leap of Life

I want to let out a blood-curdling whoop
and run around like a mad dog
or a 4-year old Indian brave.

I want to feel the blood pouring thru my veins;
Learning thru the heart;
and orgasm of blood.

Just to be alive is wonderful.
I can't sit still, I must leap and
roar just like a wild animal
let out of its cage.

Music of the Spheres

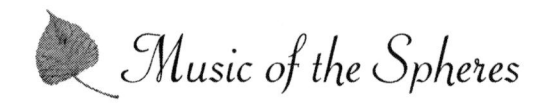

One night I had a wonderful dream.
I dreamed I heard the music of the spheres;
first faintly then louder and loudest.
it stole into my heart.

The world and I were turning over,
revolving in space and time;
the same space and time
in perfect harmony.

This separation I had always felt,
this loneliness I had been aware of
vanished for the space of this dream.

Music from the center of the earth;
from God and the solar system at the same time,
humming, ever humming.
Beautiful music of the spheres.

A wheel in a wheel
going round in the middle of the sky.
I was the center of the universe and the
universe was the center of me

I shouted to my parents,
"It's here, it's here!
I found it, I found it"!
The music of the spheres.

Soul Journey

My Blue Trunk

I see it before my eyes,
My blue trunk with gold-plated locks.
It even has a tiny key
that fits the lock.

I see my shirts in one pile with collars buttoned up.
I see my pants in another pile, resting like dried leaves.
My Father, with patient care
has labeled all my clothes;
no possible mix-up.

I have a special fold-up toothbrush in a tiny case.
I have my tortoise shell comb, how pretty it is.
I am all fixed up and ready for camp.
I close and lock my blue trunk.

Soul Journey

Nighttime Manhattan Beach

The night darkens like velvet.
I watch the surfers move with the muscle of the sea.
Moment of white foam
Splashes on the shore.
I listen to my silent heart speak.

Soul Journey
~66~

Helen Keller

The sightless and the strongest,
the quiet and the full of life.
Blind, deaf, she trods her surface of smiling eyes
into the darkness that is no darkness,
but real inner light.
By a hand of friends guided
showing her the path.
Showering petals of flowers on sunburned faces.
No one can tread your path but you.
Awake to the thunder of words
being real live images, real things, real people.
Not surpassed in beauty, not surpassed in faith.
Determination sits on her brow.
Tied to a firm mast she crashed thru
billowing water unafraid.
She dared to gaze at the sun.
Sunlight streaming from her soul,
a gift of perfect faith to us.

Song of Songs I

I am a young girl,
fresh as a lily.
The healing waters flow within me.
I bath in jasmine.
I worship the sun
as he comes riding up from beneath the horizon.
I am a doe with two bright eyes.
I am a sermon on the mount.
I lived at the time of Jezebel,
but I am comely, oh daughters of Jerusalem.
My lover waits all day for me.
He thinks of my breasts like twin peaks
where the snow has fallen the evening before.
I bound over the mountain like a young gazelle.
My lover breathes fire onto my neck.
I worship the silvery moon gliding in the sky.
My lover brings me pomegranates and dates.
We feed each other.

We lie on couches filled with myrrh.
He presses himself to me.
What wonder, what delight.
I am on fire my love, help me.
I am a burning tabernacle filled with heavy words.
Give me my inheritance from the
bosom of the earth;
from the history of Adam and Eve.
We melt as one flame.

Soul Journey

Songs of Songs II

My lover bounds over the hillside
Fresh as a deer.
He comes toward me holding red flowers in his hands.
We fall to the earth,
immortal we feel.
We breathe each other's scent.
We enfold in flames.
Our lips caress each other.
The palms of his hands are on my breast.
I feel faint, ennobled.
Erect he stands and firm.
We break the ground asunder.
Rocks issue forth, burning rock.
We have only one grave to fall into.
Even death we still love.
Fiercely the hot sun pours into us.
Showers of sparks to the heaven.
We embrace.
God issues forth in crimson robes.
He melts us together
We sigh.

Soul Journey
~72~

Seattle

Fear like a tight sheath encased me.
I came to Washington land of lakes and mountains
swimming with fish.
I gobbled blackberries by the side of the road.
I saw people sitting on front porches talking with neighbors.
In Los Angeles, there were no front porches and no neighbors.
Each person walled inside his separate oasis;
an oasis of loneliness with Hollywood bodies.
In Seattle I watched people tending plants and flowers
in the rain.
in Los Angeles there was no rain;
land of endless sunshine without seasons to circle the year.
In Washington, I feel the tang of fall and soft melon moon
floats on the lake.
Winter in Seattle can be dreary but people do not complain.
In Los Angeles people complained when a single cloud
passed over the sky.
I like the soft feathery clouds of spring.
I like the coffee and the bubble of soup in winter.
Music spills from cafes as I walk with my umbrella
down the street.
Resemblance to Europe,
reminiscent of the Orient
my cozy friendly city, Seattle.

Poetic Expressions of a Heart-Centered Life

Soul Journey

Tea

A soft spot on the tongue,
A stranger is here.
Have we taken
unusual medicine
residing in tea?
The leaves bring out
the colors of emotion
bursting like bubbles
in a hot volcano.
Deep anger rises to the surface and
vaporizes in
thinness of air.
Recording no thoughts
simply being together
with my mind
is all I ask.

Soul Journey

Loneliness

I have tramped thru fields of frozen snow.
I have walked thru ribbons of sunlight.
I have frozen feet in the snow.
I have felt the frost bite my toes.
None of these are as empty as loneliness.
None of these bite harder than the wolf.
Loneliness is the wolf at the door.
The rain, the sorrow, the sadness
of not being able to say
I am like you; we belong together.
A mast of the ship
standing forth thru waves of crested snow,
gushing thru deep waters.
But God brought me out with a strong arm
and an outstretched hand.

D. H. Lawrence

Shall I tell you a secret?
I have no lover
but there is one man whose face I secretly kiss.
He is D. H. Lawrence,
the writer, now dead.
The man who wrote Lady Chatterley's Lover
which I have memorized.
It sits in my brain like a flame
showering me with its promise of love making
in the bath of eternity.
The more I read of him
the less I comprehend.
His writing is a mystery to me;
a mystical map of universe filled with lovely flowers
and hot sun.
The more I read,
the less I understand
of the cool mint moon
and the glow of a girl.
Every night before sleep
I indulge in this ritual.

I look forward to it all day
To those few minutes alone
with my lover lying
so comforting in my arms.
He extends his long line of fiction,
so real, so real,
into the cornerstone of my brain;
into the interstices of my heart.
He tells me my dreams are real.
My true love will have only this man as his rival;
the poet, the writer,
the kink-hearted, tender Lawrence
to share my bed with me.

Soul Journey

Sleep

Wrap me in a mantle of oblivion
for I am perfect, oh God.

You made me just right,
shiny hair, flashing teeth,
limbs heavy with languor
eyelids softly closing.
Guide me into proper sleep,
The sleep of creation
where the first man and woman
gazed at one another in absolute wonder
In the Garden of Eden.
Like two jewels softly shining
without hatred and without fear.

Wrap me in a mantle of oblivion
for I am perfect, oh God.
Bundled tightly in my bed
Like a baby in its blanket.
In perfect, content,
oneness with you
Oh, the splendor of sleep.

Soul Journey

El Amor Brujo

It was a dance.
Beat loud drum.
Dance gypsy woman,
In long skirts and tight bodices.
Beat and play the melody of passion
engulfed from the grave.
One love dead, one lover living
but unfaithful in life.
He calls from the grave,
menaces her.
Echoes of pain.
She cannot sleep.
The flame is flickering higher and higher.
One man goes to prison for 4 years for a crime he didn't
commit. Ay, the pain of love,
entwining, enticing round and round it circles.
Who is its prey?
The wind howls thru the sheets at night.
Beat gypsy dance, beat.

The House of Bernarda Alba

The roof shook with the scorn of the widow.
Staff in hand she treads the floor.
My daughters do my will only in this house or die.
No men here, Bernarda.
Locked up shuttered
against the blazing noonday heat.
Heat of the bodies of 5 virgin women
From ages 39-20.
The youngest, the beauty.
The oldest, the richest.
Here comes Pepe Romano
tight buttocks and legs to
the window of the eldest promised to him.
At another window, the youngest,
panting for love at 4:30 in the morning.
The white stallion, pounding, penis erect,
fighting to get out of the stable,
thirsting for mares.

Beware Bernarda.
Watch out, watch out.
Bernarda, the spinster.

Soul Journey

No heart in her breast.
Thinks she can control life.
Bernarda's mother,
at 80 locked up in her room,
dreaming of a lover and a baby,
bathing in the cool green sea.
Watch out Bernarda
You are like a tight fist,
but stronger than your will is the
heartbeat of a passionate woman.
It broke the bond between sisters.
Now full of hate and jealously
the youngest hung herself for Pepe Romero.
You are too late Bernarda.
You will live with the hate
and it will stick in your bones.

Soul Journey
~86~

Blue Green Harmony

There is no harmony like blue green harmony.
The harmony of icy water next to sturdy trees,
straight trees, tall leafed trees.
Kings they are as I ride by.
I salute you trees of Sherwood.
I quench my thirst at the blue waters,
the ageless waters.

Soul Journey
~88~

At Home

I drove into the country today
I was not prepared to feel
comforted by cows,
stimulated by horses,
rested by farmland,
welcomed by sunflowers,
at home in a place I had never been.

Soul Journey
~90~

Vacation

On my trip
I get up at 5 am.
I am not lonely.
I am not tired.
I go all day.
I am alive.

Soul Journey
~92~

Danny Kay

Danny Kay has fun every day.
He knows a child's heart needs
protection and nourishment.
Have fun. Let's play at life, he says.
Not because it has no meaning but rather
because life has too much meaning and we need a
release from it.

Soul Journey

The Sperm Whale

Silently tiptoe the antelope.
They caress my shoulder blades.
Hold tightly together
the sinews of my soul.
Laid bare like
blades of grass,
they glisten on the sidewalk.
Gravel is everywhere, slippery.
Seals dance in the
furrows of the
silent seas.
At the zoo
the whale spouts his juice at us.
The sperm whale.

Soul Journey
~96~

Night Thoughts

Black night encompasses me.
I walk like a shadow in the deep, dark night,
alone and lonely.
I trust no one although others trust me.
Tell your secrets to the deep, dark night.
They will lie hidden there,
gleaming like gold dust to be
picked up by hungry hands later on.
Do you dare to tell the truth?
There is nobody left but me,
caged in silent isolation I write,
pain too deep to handle.
Don't talk to strangers.
Wait until dark
to tell your secrets to the moon and stars.
How to live life fully
even being unhappy?
That is the question.
It feels good to talk to the page.
Like a God I sit and write, immortal,
wrapped in oblivion lies an invisible cloak.
Let the past recede like an ocean wave
leaving only the present moment to live in.

Soul Journey
~98~

Naomi

Wings beating at the breast;
betrayal, betrayal.
Heart of lead and feathers
bent to Hell and back again in one passion.
Seated in a circle of flowers
whispering to cats.
Beauty like the dawn
breaking over the ocean.
Pure, fresh falling
Earrings.
Clothes to match the image inside
'Brave, "con huevos".
She searches the horizon.
Unusual and enigmatic.
Not yet having found the answer
or the right food.
Determined and spontaneous.
Footfalls, footfalls.
Secrets daring to break free.
Biding her time
to flash like a knife
and cut the world in half.

Soul Journey
~100~

Cell of Silence

Cell of silence.
Quiet heart awakens.
It tells me the truth about myself;
a lesson in loneliness;
face fear.

Soul Journey

Tree

I sit with my back against a swaying pine tree.
Slowly, my body gets into the rhythm of the tree itself.
We become one.
I shoot out bristles.
I feel my roots go deep into the earth.
I touch water.
I spread out my branches.
I look and feel my leaves turning yellow, red, and brown.
I have a new home;
oh, the comfort of my tree.

Soul Journey
~104~

Evil

Evil is biting the heel of goodness;
snapping at its feet like a mad dog.
Evil is the egoist
who tramples on the mystery of life.
Evil is the half-wit who fumbles
at the rising mind's consciousness.
Evil is the death-wish of my eternal soul.

Yitzhak Rabin

Black night stretches its fingers over the sky.
Dust to dust, ashes to ashes,
a great man is now dead.
Build your death ships.
A soul torn loose from its body too soon, too soon
dragged down to hell.
Oh how art the mighty fallen!
What fiendish deed is this devilment done
Israel moans in her sleep.
We wander half-naked down streets whose name
we have forgotten.
Our souls torn and tattered, we wait for the light to return.
But that light is not here anymore.
we are bereft of a friend.
Shakespeare's *Macbeth* did not do such dastardly a deed
The stench of death is in our tread.
our lungs are filled with it,
Our bellies want to vomit.
Though we feel like war inside, we must,
we must go on to Peace.

Soul Journey

The voice of God roars in the wilderness.
Shame, shame on Israel,
the beloved of God.
Shema Yisrael, Adonai Eloheynu, Adonai Echad
(Hear O' Israel, the Lord our God, the Lord in one.)

Soul Journey

Psalm

By the waters of Babylon I sat and grieved.
My head was downcast;
my heart was lead.
Then I called for my God and He rescued me
out of the flaming pit.
He took me out and put me upon his Rock;
the rock of Zion.
Then a lantern lit in my soul.
I grew stronger.
Vast, vast is the power of the mind.
I am a cathedral
with a burning lamp
shining thru the night;
shining thru the centuries.
Now I am lit up from within.
Like a ship my compass is set.
Like a tower with bells ringing.
I am nothing yet I am everything.
I see both behind and beyond.
I grow with the lamp in my soul.

Soul Journey
~110~

Prayer: Let Me Be Always Near You

God, let me be always near you. Let me understand
that we are partners, you and I,
in this journey thru life and that as I travel thru I come closer
to you. Let me take your hand. Guide me closer to my dreams.
You and I are moving together to make my dreams become real.
The more I love you, the more I value myself. The more I rely
on you, the stronger I get. You have given me dignity.
You have shown me your love.
Thank you, Dear Father.

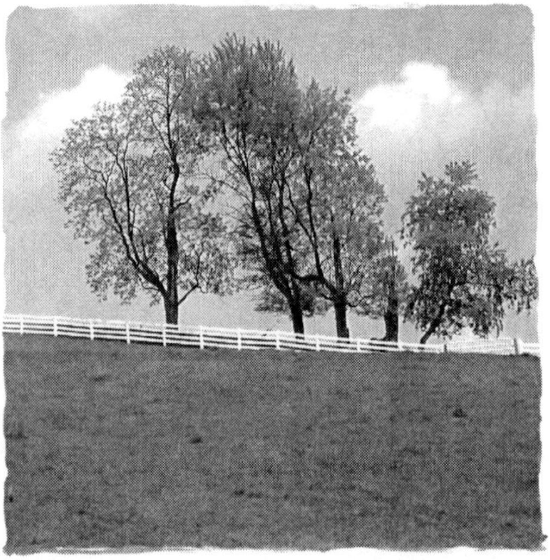

Prayer of Comfort

Dear God,

Let me be enveloped in your loving ways. Let me be guided by your light. When anguish comes, be my friend and comfort me. When I make mistakes, help me to learn from them. Teach me to be patient with disappointments, always remembering that things happen in your time frame and that to everything there is a season, a time, and a purpose. Help me to see myself as happy and healthy, just as you made me. Show me that I am always part of you, dear Father.

Amen.

Soul Journey
~114~

Helpmate Prayer

Dear God,
Teach me how to value myself. As one of your creatures, show me that I have dignity and self-worth. You have been kind to me; show me how to be kind to myself. You have shown me that I am important to you; show me that I am important to myself. Be thou my cherished friend. Be thou like a lover to me. Join hands with me. Be thou my helpmate in time of trouble. Do not Forget me. Teach me how to love and be loved.

Soul Journey

A Prayer

Thank you dear Lord,
You made the world just right.
Everything in harmony, if
we can but see it whole.
The rhythm, the joy,
The coming out, the coming inside.
Friends, lights, candles, in
the dark space illumination.
Our soul.
The world is for us, when we feel it so,
hug for joy the human beings in the street,
for we were made in your image;
Yours and ours combined.
There is no You with us.
There is no us with You.
Gentle harmony space.
A pause that connects.
Oneness.

Author Biography

I was born in Carmel-by-the-Sea, California. I have almost always lived by the water, and it has been a source of serenity, beauty, and creativity to me. As a young child, I used to derive great pleasure from drawing designs in rapturous colors, and my painting in later years also followed this style. Flowers have always meant a great deal to me, and I would photograph them lovingly, in a non-professional manner. Trees also have grounded me and there are many poems in this book written in homage to trees.

I came to Seattle, Washington in 1996 to escape big city living and to find a community more in harmony with nature and less superficial than Hollywood, California. I fell in love with Seattle; its mountains, its lakes, its Puget sound. I only found the winter season to be somewhat gray and dark.

I always wanted a marriage and family life and have not given up on that dream, although I am now 55 years old. I have always loved children and have spent most of my life working with them in one form or another, whether in preschool or in afterschool programs. I once volunteered at Children's Hospital where, for 6 months, I played the guitar for the children there. I love music and go to the symphony often. I also enjoy several forms of jazz music. I have a sister who lives in San Rafael, California, where she teaches Feldekrais body alignment.

When I am not writing poetry or engaged in music, I spend a good deal of my time searching for very unique candles, which I offer for sale through my website: www.TheElegantCandle.net.